Sports Illustrated KID$

STARS OF SPORTS

T0025630

CHRISTIAN YELICH

BASEBALL MVP

by *Matt Chandler*

CAPSTONE PRESS
a capstone imprint

Published by Capstone Press, an imprint of Capstone
1710 Roe Crest Drive, North Mankato, Minnesota 56003
capstonepub.com

Library of Congress Cataloging-in-Publication Data
Names: Chandler, Matt, author. Title: Christian Yelich : baseball MVP / Matt Chandler.
Description: North Mankato, Minnesota : Capstone Press, an imprint of Capstone. [2022] | Series: Sports Illustrated Kids stars
of sports | Includes bibliographical references and index. | Audience: Ages 8-11 | Audience: Grades 4-6 | Summary: "Outfielder
Christian Yelich joined Little League when he was four and never stopped playing. From traveling teams when he was young
to being drafted as a professional player, baseball was a priority for Yelich. He was named the National League's MVP in 2018.
Read on to find out more about Yelich's amazing baseball career"—Provided by publisher. Identifiers: LCCN 2021028243
(print) | LCCN 2021028244 (ebook) | ISBN 9781663983602 (hardcover) | ISBN 9781666323153 (paperback) | ISBN
9781666323160 (pdf) | ISBN 9781666323184 (kindle edition) Subjects: LCSH: Yelich, Christian, 1991—Juvenile literature. |
Outfielders (Baseball)—United States—Biography—Juvenile literature. | Baseball players—United States—Biography—Juvenile
literature. | Most Valuable Player Award (Baseball)—Juvenile literature. | Milwaukee Brewers (Baseball team)—History—
Juvenile literature. | Major League Baseball (Organization)—History—Juvenile literature. Classification: LCC GV865.Y43 C43
2022 (print) | LCC GV865.Y43 (ebook) | DDC 796.357092 [B]—dc23 LC record available at https://lccn.loc.gov/2021028243
LC ebook record available at https://lccn.loc.gov/2021028244

Editorial Credits
Editor: Christianne Jones; Designer: Bobbie Nuytten; Media Researcher: Morgan Walters; Production Specialist: Laura Manthe

Image Credits
Associated Press: Carlos Osorio, 28, Jeffrey Phelps, 6, Keith Srakocic, 18, Mark J. Terrill, 7, Mike Janes/Four Seam Images, 16,
17, Tom DiPace, 11, Tony Farlow/Four Seam Images, 12, 15; Getty Images: Gary Friedman, 9, Rob Foldy/Miami Marlins, 25;
John Fisher/Cal Sport Media, Cover, 22, Kyodo, 21, Larry Radloff/Icon Sportswire DGO, 5, 26, Lawrence Iles/Icon Sportswire
DKI, 23, 27; Shutterstock: Eugene Onischenko, 1; Sports Illustrated: Erick W. Rasco, 13

Source Notes
Page 7, "Everything I've done…," Christian Yelich, "This is for all the Baseball Moms," The Players Tribune,
May 9, 2019, https://www.theplayerstribune.com, Accessed July 18, 2021.
Page 7, "From that point…," Christian Yelich, "This is for all the Baseball Moms," The Players Tribune,
May 9, 2019, https://www.theplayerstribune.com, Accessed July 18, 2021.
Page 8, "He was the…," Lori Nickel, "Christian Yelich embraces 'return' to Brewers," Milwaukee Journal Sentinel,
May 3, 2018, https://www.jsonline.com, Accessed July 18, 2021.
Page 11, "odd throwing motion…," Matt Blue, "Scouting Florida Marlins 2010: First round draft pick Christian
Yelich," Bleacher Report, July 21, 2010, https://bleacherreport.com, Accessed July 18, 2021.
Page 13, "It was a tough…," Jorge Milian, "Top pick Christian Yelich picked Marlins over UM," The Palm Beach
Post, August 22, 2010, https://www.palmbeachpost.com, Accessed July 18, 2021.
Page 14, "All the teams…," Brian Biggane, "Miami Marlins see similarities between Jupiter Hammerheads
prospect Christian Yelich and Washington Nationals' Bryce Harper," The Palm Beach Post, May 14, 2012,
https://www.palmbeachpost.com, Accessed July 18, 2021.
Page 17, "He can do a…," Brian Biggane, "Miami Marlins see similarities between Jupiter Hammerheads
prospect Christian Yelich and Washington Nationals' Bryce Harper," The Palm Beach Post, May 14, 2012,
https://www.palmbeachpost.com, Accessed July 18, 2021.
Page 20, "I'm excited about…," Associated Press, "Christian Yelich signs 7-year contract," ESPN, March 22, 2015,
https://www.espn.com, Accessed July 18, 2021.
Page 21, "I didn't get…," Jon Paul Morosi, "Yelich honored to be on Team USA for World Baseball Classic,"
Major League Baseball, December 19, 2016, https://www.mlb.com, Accessed July 18, 2021.

TABLE OF CONTENTS

Words in **BOLD** are in the glossary.

Milwaukee Brewers left fielder Christian Yelich walked slowly to the plate on September 17, 2018. It was the bottom of the sixth inning and 32,145 fans stood and cheered wildly. The Brewers led the Cincinnati Reds 6–0. Yelich was 3-for-3 in the game. He needed only a triple to hit through the **cycle**.

Reds pitcher Jesus Reyes delivered a slider low and inside. Yelich turned and drove the ball to the gap in right center field. The ball rolled to the wall and Yelich raced to third base. The triple gave him his second cycle of the season! Yelich drove in four runs and led his team to the win, 8–0. Yelich became only the fifth player in the history of baseball to hit through two cycles in one season.

FACT

Yelich became the only player in history to hit through the cycle twice in a season against the same team. Just three weeks earlier, on August 30, 2018, he hit his first cycle against the Reds.

Christian Stephen Yelich was born on December 5, 1991, in Thousand Oaks, California. He has two younger brothers, Collin and Cameron. Yelich didn't come from a baseball background. His uncle, Chris Yelich, and his great-grandfather, Fred Gehrke, both played football.

Growing up, Yelich credits his mom Alecia with helping make him a baseball star. She always encouraged him to play. She drove Yelich to practice and to games and tournaments across California.

>>> Yelich hugs his mother before a 2019 game.

"Everything I've done up to this point as a player, everything I'm doing now, and everything I do in the future," Yelich said, "all of that would've been wiped away if my mom wouldn't have cared as much as she did back then."

Yelich's brother Collin also loved baseball. The two boys grew up playing the game together. Collin also went on to play professional baseball in the Atlanta Braves organization.

Moneyball

When he first began playing as a boy, Yelich got hit by pitches—a lot. He came home from a game one day and told his mom he was quitting baseball. Then his mom had an idea. She offered him $5 if he got a hit in his next game. It worked. Yelich got a hit and mom paid up. "And then from that point forward, for whatever reason, I was never worried about being hit by a pitch again. After I put the ball in play that one time it was like, Hey, look . . . everything's going to be fine with baseball," he said.

HIGH SCHOOL HERO

After playing Little League, Yelich was ready for high school baseball. Many freshmen start out on the junior **varsity** team. Once they get more experience, they join the varsity team. Yelich was so good he played on the varsity team all four years of high school.

Today, Yelich is considered one of the best outfielders in baseball. But in high school, he played first base and third base for the Westlake High School Warriors.

Yelich was an amazing batter. He hit .416 for his high school career. He smacked 20 home runs. Yelich also showed off his speed, stealing 65 bases over four seasons.

Corey Rodriguez was a major league **scout** in California who watched Yelich during his high school career. "He was the most talented kid on the high school field whenever he went out there," Rodriguez said.

> >>> Yelich watches the action on the field during a Westlake High game in 2008.

FACT

Yelich was teammates with his brother Collin for two seasons on the Westlake Warriors.

CHAPTER TWO

A HARD CHOICE

Yelich saved his best for last. In his senior year at Westlake, he was unstoppable. He hit .451 with 14 doubles and nine home runs in just 82 at bats.

Westlake High School was known for having a great baseball team over the years. Several players had already gone on to play in the major leagues. That meant a lot of scouts were at the games to see Yelich play.

The scouting report on Yelich was that he was a great hitter with excellent speed. Even though he played infield positions, scouts believed he could be moved to the outfield.

The one weakness in his game was his arm. He had what one scout called an "odd throwing motion." Still, he was expected to be drafted straight out of high school to play professional baseball!

>>> Yelich's unique throwing style didn't keep him from being a star player.

MARLIN OR HURRICANE?

Yelich was **recruited** to play baseball for the University of Miami Hurricanes. But on June 7, 2010, the Florida Marlins selected Yelich as the 23rd pick in the Major League Baseball Draft. He had a decision to make.

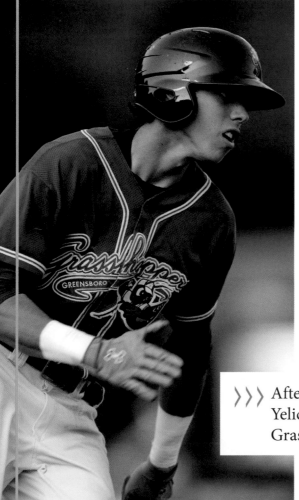

Going to college would give him a free education. It would also allow him to grow physically and improve as a player. However, as a first-round pick, Yelich would become an instant millionaire if he signed with the Marlins.

〉〉〉 After signing with the Marlins, Yelich played for the Greensboro Grasshoppers **minor league** team.

"It was a tough decision," Yelich said. "I've wanted to be a professional baseball player. It's been a dream of mine since I was 4 years old."

In the end, he followed his dream. The Marlins signed Yelich to a rookie contract that included a $1.7 million signing **bonus**.

FACT

Yelich grew up in California and attended games at Dodger Stadium. But his favorite player as a kid was New York Yankees shortstop Derek Jeter.

LIFE AS A PRO

After signing his contract, Yelich was assigned to the Marlins minor league team in the Gulf Coast League. He played in just 12 games his first year in professional baseball. Still, he hit an impressive .362.

The Marlins immediately switched Yelich to the outfield. They thought his speed would make him a great center fielder. The rookie wasn't surprised.

"All the teams I talked to (before the draft) were planning to convert me to outfield," Yelich said. "Center is my favorite position."

Even though it was a new position for him, Yelich didn't make any errors in his first season. Just a few months earlier, Yelich was a high school first baseman getting ready to go to college. Now, he was a professional outfielder getting paid to play!

Yelich began the 2011 season with the Greensboro Grasshoppers, the Marlins Class-A team in North Carolina. In 122 games he hit 15 home runs and drove in 77 runs.

>>> With the Grasshoppers, Yelich gained the skills he needed for future success.

In 2012, the Marlins moved Yelich up in their minor league system. He played for the Jupiter Hammerheads. Yelich began the season as the top **prospect** in the Marlins organization. His new manager in Jupiter, Andy Haines, believed Yelich had everything it took to be a star.

〉〉〉 Playing for the Jupiter Hammerheads minor league team helped Yelich master his skills.

"He can do a little bit of everything," Haines said in 2012. "He's a pure hitter, hit for power, good defensive player, run the bases."

Yelich hit .329 for the Hammerheads. He also showed off his speed, stealing 20 bases. Yelich was developing into a major league player. His 2012 season in Jupiter would be his last full season in the minor leagues.

››› Yelich plays in the outfield during a Jupiter Hammerheads game in July 2012.

FACT

Yelich throws right-handed, but he bats left-handed.

MAJOR LEAGUER

After spending three years in the minors, on July 23, 2013, the Marlins promoted Yelich to the majors. His **debut** was against the Colorado Rockies. In his first major league at bat, Yelich ripped a single to right field off Rockies starter Jhoulys Chacín. He finished his first game going 2-for-4 at the plate.

Two weeks later, on August 8, against the Pittsburgh Pirates, Yelich hit his first career home run. With a runner on second, Yelich swung hard at the pitch from Gerrit Cole. He hit a high fly ball deep to left field. Pirates left fielder Alex Presley gave chase, but it landed in the bleachers! Yelich finished his rookie season appearing in 62 games for the Marlins.

TOUGH TIMES IN MIAMI

Yelich spent four more seasons in Miami. In 2014, he became the youngest player in Marlins history to win a Gold Glove.

Yelich showed steady improvement as a hitter, but the team never made the playoffs. As a first-round draft pick, the team had high expectations for Yelich. He was drafted for his ability to hit, but he never had a 25 home-run season as a Marlin. He never drove in 100 runs in a season either. His batting average was below .300.

He was a very solid player, but he wasn't developing into the superstar many people expected. Still, just before the start of the 2015 season, the Marlins signed him to a seven-year, $49.5 million contract.

"I'm excited about the direction we're headed," Yelich told ESPN in an interview after signing the contract. "It's great to have a good team now and in the future."

World Baseball Classic

Yelich says he always dreamed of representing the United States in a global competition.

"I didn't get a chance in high school and then I signed with the Marlins after my senior year, so I couldn't do it in college, either," he said.

In 2017, he finally got his chance. Yelich was chosen to be part of Team USA and competed in the World Baseball Classic. Yelich hit .310 in the WBC. He scored seven runs to help lead the United States to victory!

⟩⟩⟩ Yelich hits a single in the World Baseball Classic in Los Angeles in 2017.

CHAPTER FOUR

FROM MIAMI TO MILWAUKEE

On January 25, 2018, the Miami Marlins shocked the baseball world. The team traded Yelich to the Milwaukee Brewers for four players. Yelich was coming off two solid seasons in Miami. He hit a combined 39 home runs and drove in 179 runs in 2016 and 2017. But the Marlins saw a chance to build their team with four young players.

〉〉〉 Lorenzo Cain congratulates Yelich on a two-run homer in a game against the Philadelphia Phillies in 2018.

In Miami, Yelich played in a half-empty stadium many nights. The Marlins were bad. In his five seasons with Miami, the team never had a winning record. In 2013, his rookie season, they lost 100 games.

The trade to the Brewers was career changing for Yelich. In Milwaukee, the Brewers were coming off an 86-win season. There was plenty of talent, and Yelich was seen as the final piece of the puzzle.

〉〉〉 Yelich hits in a 2018 game against the Cincinnati Reds.

MVP SEASON

Yelich had been unhappy in Miami. He wanted to be traded to a team where he had a chance to win. Milwaukee gave him that chance, and he took advantage of it. Yelich had been a solid player in Miami. In Milwaukee, he suddenly exploded.

The Brewers opened the season with a three-game series against the San Diego Padres. Yelich crushed Padres pitching, hitting .500 in the series and helping his team sweep San Diego.

Yelich never slowed down. He finished the season batting .326 and winning the Tony Gwynn National League Batting Champion Award. He hit 36 home runs and drove in 110 runs. Both were career bests. Defensively, Yelich played all three outfield positions. He finished the season with only three errors in 147 games! His tremendous season earned him the National League Most Valuable Player Award (MVP).

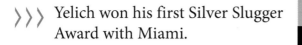

〉〉〉 Yelich won his first Silver Slugger Award with Miami.

FACT

Yelich earned his second Silver Slugger Award in 2018. The award is given to the best offensive player at each position in the league.

CHAPTER FIVE

MONSTER CONTRACT

After back-to-back monster years in 2018 and 2019, the Brewers wanted to lock in their superstar. In 2020, the Brewers signed Yelich to a nine-year, $215 million contract. It was the largest contract in the history of the team.

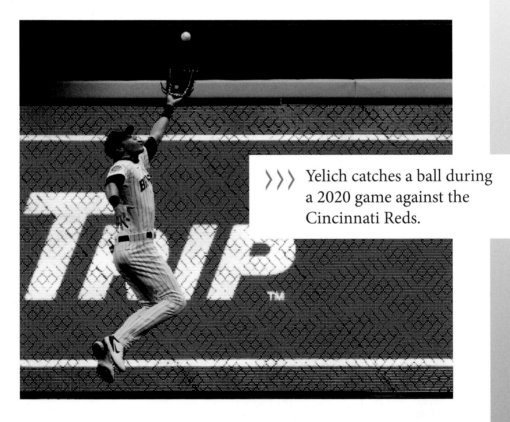

〉〉〉 Yelich catches a ball during a 2020 game against the Cincinnati Reds.

Unfortunately, **COVID-19** had a huge impact on the 2020 baseball season. Major League Baseball shortened the season. Teams played only 60 games instead of the usual 162. Yelich responded with the worst season of his career. In 2019, Yelich's batting average was .329. In 2020, he hit just .205. He finished the 60-game season with only 12 home runs and 22 runs batted in. The Brewers finished the shortened season with a losing record of 29–31.

〉〉〉 Yelich smashes a home run in a game against the Kansas City Royals in 2020.

PREDICTING THE FUTURE

Yelich's young career has been up and down. He started off slow in his first seasons with the Florida Marlins. He became a superstar in Milwaukee. Then, after signing the biggest contract in team history, he had his worst season. Yelich has to be more **consistent**. If he can do that, he may be leading a World Series parade in Milwaukee soon!

〉〉〉 Yelich at bat against the Detroit Tigers in 2020.

TIMELINE

1991   Christian Yelich is born in Thousand Oaks, California, on December 5.

2010   Yelich is offered a scholarship to play baseball for the University of Miami Hurricanes.

2010   Yelich is selected in the first round of the Major League Baseball Draft by the Florida Marlins.

2013   Yelich makes his Major League debut for the Marlins on July 23.

2014   Yelich becomes the youngest player in Marlins history to win a Gold Glove.

2018   The Marlins trade Yelich to the Milwaukee Brewers on January 25.

2018   Yelich wins the National League MVP Award.

2020   The Brewers sign Yelich to a nine-year, $215 million contract extension.

GLOSSARY

BONUS (BOH-nuhss)—extra money a worker receives for doing a good job

CONSISTENT (kuhn-SIS-tuhnt)—always behaving in the same way

COVID-19 (KOH-vid nine-TEEN)—a very contagious and sometimes deadly virus that spread worldwide in 2020

CYCLE (SI-kul)—hitting a single, double, triple, and home run in the same game

DEBUT (DAY-byoo)—a first showing

MINOR LEAGUE (MYE-nur LEEG)—a league of teams where players improve their skills before joining a major league team

PROSPECT (pros-PEKT)—a potential candidate

RECRUIT (ri-KROOT)—to ask someone to join a company or organization

SCOUT (SKOWT)—someone who looks for players who might be able to be professionals

VARSITY (VAR-si-tee)—the main team representing a high school or college in a sport or other competition

READ MORE

Chandler, Matt. *Baseball's Greatest Walk-Offs and Other Crunch-Time Heroics*. North Mankato, MN: Capstone, 2020.

Doeden, Matt. *It's Outta Here!: The Might and Majesty of the Home Run*. Minneapolis: Millbrook Press, 2021.

Rajczak, Michael. *The Greatest Baseball Players of All Time*. New York: Gareth Stevens Publishing, 2020.

INTERNET SITES

ESPN Bio: Christian Yelich
espn.com/mlb/player/_/id/31283/christian-yelich

MLB: Christian Yelich #22
mlb.com/player/christian-yelich-592885

MLB: Milwaukee Brewers
mlb.com/brewers

INDEX

AUTHOR BIO

Matt Chandler is the author of more than 60 books for children and thousands of articles published in newspapers and magazines. He writes mostly nonfiction books with a focus on sports, ghosts and haunted places, and graphic novels. Matt lives in New York.